99 x Austrian Cooking
by Helga Setz

Helga Setz

99 x
Austrian Cooking

Heyn

Translated by Helga Setz

© by Verlag Johannes Heyn
Druck: Kohlweis
Klagenfurt, 1989
ISBN 3 85366 579 9

Introduction – Austrian Cooking

Austrian Cooking has a great variety of dishes – a heritage of the once great Austrian Empire. In the Austrian Provinces there are many native traditions. The people of the Provinces were not wealthy and ate what was available in the surrounding country. So these dishes are very simple, tasty, substantial and cheap. Moreover in terms of current interests they also fit todays need for a proper healthy diet. It was completely different in bigger towns. In the towns there has always been a lively exchange of culinary ideas with other areas. First of all Vienna was a focal meeting place for the Empire and its peoples. Many Viennese residents were wealthy. They could afford expensive food and the cuisine became more and more sophisticated and refined. In this way many good dishes, not originally Austrian, became naturalizised. Today they are a permanent part of Austrian Cuisine.

With this small book I have tried to give you a modest selection of typical Austrian dishes. I felt that our guests from abroad who appreciate Austrian Cuisine should be able to cook Austrian dishes at home. That presupposes that the necessary ingredients are available in other countries and that the preparation of the dishes is not too complicated. These were further criteria for the selection of dishes I have presented here.

However the skill and understanding of the cook is critical to the translation of the prosaic language of a recipe into a real delight to the palate.

All recipes unless otherwise mentioned are for 4 persons. Excepted are the sweets and puddings. Here it is almost impossible to produce tasty dishes with such small amounts. Castor sugar should be used for these dishes.
1 tsp = 1 teaspoon, 1 Tbs = 1 tablespoon
I hope you enjoy cooking these dishes as much as I do.

Helga Setz

Soups

Beef Broth
Rindsuppe

600 g (21 oz) of beef with bones
100 g (3½ oz) pot herbs (carrot, celeriac, leek, parsnip)
1 small onion
1½ l (2½ pt) water
5 peppercorns
mace
1 tsp salt
chopped chives

Put meat, bones, roughly chopped pot herbs, onion, spices in a saucepan cover with cold water. Bring to the boil and simmer slowly for 1½ hours. Strain, season and serve with dumplings noodles etc. and chopped chives.

The meat may be eaten with potatoes, vegetables, chive sauce or apple-horse-radish sauce. Cold meat can also be used for beef salad.

Liver Dumplings
Leberknödel

150 g (5½ oz) liver, finely minced
1 roll
1 Tbs cooking fat
50 g (2 oz) onion
1 tsp parsley
1 clove garlic
a little marjoram, thyme, basil
1 tsp salt
1 egg
app. 60 g (2 oz) breadcrumbs

Soak the roll in water and squeeze it out. Brown the finely chopped onion in fat, stir in chopped parsley and crushed garlic.
Mix all ingredients into a dough. Form 4 big or 8 small dumplings. Simmer them in boiling broth or salted water for 10 minutes.

Serve in broth with chopped chives.

Semolina Nockerln
Grießnockerln

50 g (2 oz) butter
1 egg
100 g (3½ oz)
semolina
1 pinch nutmeg
½ tsp salt
salted water

First beat butter very creamy. Stir in other ingredients. Allow to stand for ½ hour. Scoop out small longish (1 inch) dumplings with a teaspoon. Drop into boiling salted water, simmer ½ hour.

Serve in beef broth.

Sliced Pancakes
Frittaten-Flädle

⅛ l (4 fluid oz) milk
½ tsp salt
80 g (3 oz) flour
1 egg

_____

fat for frying

Mix the cold milk and flour into a batter. Stir in egg and salt. Heat some fat in a frying pan. Pour into the pan enough batter to cover the bottom thinly and evenly. Fry on both sides until crisp. Add more fat to pan before frying next pancake. When cold, the pancakes are rolled up and cut into thin strips.

Serve separately with hot beef broth.

"Drop in Noodles"

Eintropfsuppe – Eingußnudeln

1 l (1 ¾ pt) beef
broth

Batter:
2 Tbs flour
1 egg
1 egg white
2 pinches salt

---

chopped chives

In a jug with a spout make a thin batter of flour, eggs and salt: Allow small drops of batter to fall into simmering broth. When they rise to the surface, immediately serve the soup with chives.

Biscuits
Schöberln

50 g (2 oz) butter
2 egg yolks
2 stale rolls
1 tsp cooking fat
1 tsp parsley, finely chopped
2 egg whites
½ tsp salt

Soak the rolls in water, squeeze it out and pass through a sieve. Fry parsley in fat (2 sec.). Beat butter and yolks until they are creamy. Now add rolls, parsley. Finally fold in the stiffly beaten egg whites. Put the paste into a greased and floured baking dish. Bake in a medium oven for 30 minutes until golden brown.
Cut into diamond shapes and serve with hot beef broth.

Ham Biscuits – Schinkenschöberln

Mix the paste with 100 g (3½ oz) cooked, chopped ham.

Liver Biscuits – Leberschöberln

Mix the paste with 1 Tbs onions, chopped and fried, a little marjoram, pepper and 100 g (3½ oz) liver finely minced.

Goulash Soup
Gulaschsuppe

50 g (2 oz) lard
200 g (7 oz) onion
1 clove garlic
500 g (18 oz) diced beef
1 Tbs paprika
1 Tbs tomato-purée
1 Tbs vinegar
1 tsp salt
marjoram
caraway-seeds
1 l (1¾ pt) water
250 g (9 oz) raw potatoes
1 tsp flour

Fry finely chopped onions and crushed garlic until brown: Add meat and spices. Cover with water and simmer until tender. Then add small diced potatoes. Mix flour with a little cold water, add it and cook until the potatoes are done.
Add 1 hot green pepper thinly sliced if a hot soup is preferred.

In Burgenland they cook small dumplings – Nockerln (⅓ of the dough) in the finished soup. They serve the soup with each individual dish garnished with 1 Tbs sour cream.

Styrian Klachl Soup
Steirische Klachlsuppe

2–3 small legs of pork
100 g (3½ oz) pot herbs
(carrot, leek, celeriac, sprigs of parsley)
2 bay leafs
1 tsp marjoram
5 peppercorns
2 cloves garlic
1 tsp salt
1¼ l (2 pt) water

---

1 Tbs vinegar
1 Tbs flour

Let the butcher cut the pork bones into small slices (as thick as your thumb). Cook the bones with sliced vegetables and spices in salted water until done.
Bone the meat, dice it, return to soup. Thicken with flour and season with vinegar.

Serve it with boiled potatoes.

Carinthian Festival Soup
Kärntner Kirchtagssuppe

Meat Stock:
200 g (7 oz) mutton
200 g (7 oz) beef
400 g (14 oz)
chicken
500 g (18 oz) beef
bones
1 tsp salt
50 g (2 oz) leeks
sprigs of parsley
1½ l (3 pt) water

Herb Stock:
½ l (1 pt) water
5 peppercorns
5 cloves
4 pinches saffron
1 sage leaf
2 bay leafs
1 tsp mixed spices

⅛ l (4 fluid oz) sour
cream
2 raw egg yolks
1 Tbs flour

Meat Stock: cover in a pan meat, bones, pot herbs with salted cold water and cook gently. When the meat is done, bone and slice in small pieces. Strain the soup.

Herb Stock: cover all spices with ½ l of cold water, simmer 1 hour and strain.

Mix meat stock, meat, herb stock and reboil. Stir in sour cream mixed with egg yolks and flour. Reheat, but dont boil. This soup should taste slightly sour and spicy.

It will be served with fried bread cubes or "Drop in Noodles".

Mushroom Soup
Schwammerlsuppe

40 g (1½ oz) butter
40 g (1½ oz) onion
1 clove garlic,
crushed
250 g (9 oz)
mushrooms
½ tsp marjoram
1 Tbs parsley,
chopped
¾ l (1¼ pt) water
100 g (3½ oz)
potatoes

———————

⅛ l (4 fluid oz) sour
cream
1 Tbs flour
1 tsp salt

Fry shopped onions and garlic gently in butter.
Clean, wash and cut the mushrooms. Mix them with onions. Simmer for 5 minutes. Add water, herbs, peeled, cubed potatoes and cook until soft.
Mix sour cream with flour, pour into the soup and bring to boil. Add salt to taste.

In Styria people cook this soup without potatoes. They eat buckwheat Sterz (Heidensterz) and mushroom soup together.

Garlic Soup
Knoblauchsuppe

100 g (3½ oz) bacon
10 clove garlic
100 g (3½ oz) leek
or onion, chopped
1 l (1¾ pt) water

⅛ l (4 fluid oz) sour
cream
1 raw egg yolk
1 tsp flour
½ cube of beef stock
½ tsp salt

100 g (3½ oz) bread
cut to cubes, fried

Fry finely chopped bacon, add crushed garlic and refry quickly. Stir in leek or onions, cook for 5 minutes. Add the water, simmer gently for 20 minutes.

Mix sour cream with yolk and flour. Pour this mixture into the soup and cook gently until soup thickens.

Season and serve with fried breadcubes.

Notices:

Main dishes — Meat — Offal — Fish

Boiled "Table" Beef
Gekochter Tafelspitz

Austrian "Table" Beef is cut from the top side, it is lean and fine grained.

600 g (21 oz) beef
50 g (2 oz) ox liver
2 beef bones (150 g
– 5 oz)
100 g (3½ oz) pot
herbs
(carrot, parsnip,
stalk of celery, leek)
1 tsp salt
5 peppercorns
mace
1½ (2½ pt) water

Put bones in cold water, bring to the boil. Add meat, liver, roughly chopped pot herbs, spices. Cook until tender (1½–2 hours).
Serve the meat sliced with either a hot vegetable such as spinach, cabbage etc. or a hot sauce such as bread-horse-radish or a cold sauce such as chives or apple – horse-radish. Serve with fried potatoes.

Braised Beef
Rindsbraten

800 g (1¾ lb) beef
(top side)
100 g (3½ oz) bacon
50 g (2 oz) cooking
fat
1 tsp salt
2 pinches pepper
50 g (2 oz) onions
50 g (2 oz) celeriac
50 g (2 oz) carrots
1 glass of red wine
1 bay leaf
5 pepper- and 5
pimento corns
½ tsp basil
½ tsp marjoram
1 Tbs mustard

⅛ l (4 fluid oz) sour
cream
1 Tbs flour

Cut bacon in strips (1 cm thick, 4 cm long). Cut holes in the meat and stuff them with the baconstrips. Rub the meat with salt and pepper. Heat fat in a saucepan, put in the meat. Fry over a hot flame until it is brown all over. Lift out the meat and fry in the same pan thinly sliced vegetables and onions until slightly brown. Add wine, meat, spices and just enough water or stock to moisten. Put on a tightly fitting lid and simmer gently in the oven for app. 1½ hours.

Take the meat out of the gravy and slice.

Mix cream with flour, thicken the gravy and sieve.

Serve the meatslices with the sauce, noodles, dumplings, roast potatoes, polenta slices, red cabbage etc.

Onion Steak
Zwiebelrostbraten

4 steaks of 200 g
(7 oz) each
1 tsp salt
2 pinches pepper
2 Tbs flour
40 g (1½ oz) lard

---

30 g (1 oz) butter
1 tsp flour
¼ l (8 fluid oz) water
or stock

---

200 g (7 oz) onions
1 Tbs flour
2 pinches salt

---

fat for frying

Beat the meat, nick the edges to stop them curling up while frying, season. Coat one side with flour. Heat fat in a saucepan, fry the steaks quickly on both sides (the floured side first). Keep it warm, while the gravy is prepared. Add butter to the frying fat, brown flour in it and cook it briefly with water or stock. Pour the gravy over steaks sprinkle with fried brown onionrings and serve.

For onionrings cut onions in thin slices, coat with salted flour and fry in hot fat.

Side dishes are fried or roast potatoes.

Goulash
Saftgulasch

800 g (1¾ lb) beef (leg)
100 g (3½ oz) lard
500 g (18 oz) onions
2 cloves garlic
3 Tbs paprika
1 Tbs vinegar
½ tsp marjoram
½ tsp caraway-seeds
1 Tbs tomato-purée
1 tsp salt
water as required

Cut the meat in 1–2 inch cubes, the onions in very thin slices. Fry onions in hot lard unil golden brown, mix in paprika and vinegar. Add meat, crushed garlic and all other spices and cover with water. Allow to stew slowly until the meat is tender and a smooth gravy is made (2–3 hours).

Fresh rolls and a glass of cool beer go well with it.

Vienna Cutlet
Wiener Schnitzel

*4 fillets veal, each
150 g (5 oz)
1 tsp salt*

---

*60 g (2 oz) flour
2 eggs
100 g (3½ oz)
breadcrumbs
fat for frying,
originally lard*

Lightly pound the fillets, nick the edges, salt. Coat with flour, dip in beaten egg and breadcrumbs.

Fry the fillets on both sides in deep hot fat (each side app. 1½ min.) until golden brown. Shake the pan occasionally. Serve immediately with lemon slices and parsley.

Typical Austrian side dishes are: Lettuce – potato – cucumber – or mixed salad.

Escalopes of Veal
Naturschnitzel

4 fillets veal, each
150 g (5 oz)
1 tsp salt
2 Tbs flour
50 g (2 oz) fat

---

50 g (2 oz) butter
1 Tbs flour
¼ l (½ pt) beef stock

Lightly pound the fillets, nick the edges, salt and cover one side with flour. Heat fat in a saucepan, put in the fillets with the floured side first. Quickly fry brown on both sides. Keep it warm.

Pour off the frying fat. Put butter in the pan, brown the flour, stir in the stock, cook for app. 5 minutes. Pour the juice over the fillets, serve with lemon slices and parsley.

Side dishes are: Cooked rice, plain or with green peas or button mushrooms and lettuce.

Roast Pork
Schweinsbraten

800 g (1¾ lb) pork (loin)
1 tsp salt
2 cloves garlic
1 tsp caraway-seeds
½ tsp thyme
water

Rub the meat with the spices. Pour cold water into a saucepan to 1 cm height, add meat. Braise it covered with a lid for ½ hour, then roast uncovered the next ½ hour in a hot oven. Baste it frequently. Serve the gravy with the sliced meat.

The best side dishes are: Potatoes roasted in the gravy and sauerkraut.

Stuffed Breast of Veal
Gefüllte Kalbsbrust
Serves 6

1½ kg (3 lb) breast
of veal
500 g (1 lb) cut calf
bones
1 tsp salt
50 g (2 oz) butter
¼ l (8 fluid oz) water

Stuffing:
40 g (1½ oz) butter
30 g (1 oz) onions
1 tsp chopped
parsley
100 g (3½ oz)
button
mushrooms
3 stale rolls
⅛ l (4 fluid oz) milk
2 eggs
1 pinch nutmeg
2 pinches salt

Tell the butcher to bone the
meat. To prepare the veal for
stuffing separate on the narrow
side upper meaty parts joined
with a thin membrane to form a
pocket. Stuff this pocket with
the following stuffing, stitch together, rub with salt.

Place the bones in a frying pan,
put the stuffed breast on it, dot
with butter. Quickly roast in a
hot oven, pour water on the
bones, roast for 1½ hours, bast-
ing frequently. Allow the meat
to rest ½ hour before cutting into
slices.

Mix flour and water, pour into
roasting fat, cook app. 5 min.
Sieve this gravy and serve separately.

Stuffing: Fry finely chopped
onions in butter, add thinly
sliced button mushrooms and

1 tsp flour
¼ l (8 fluid oz) water

parsley, cook for 5 min. Cut rolls to 1 cm cubes. Mix milk, eggs and spices, pour over rolls. Stir in mushrooms.

Green peas, carrots, lettuce or mixed salad go well with it.

Szeged Goulash
Szegediner Gulasch

500 g (1 lb) pork
(spare ribs or belly)
50 g (2 oz) lard
200 g (7 oz) onions
2 cloves garlic
1 Tbs paprika
½ tsp caraway-seeds
½ tsp salt
500 g (1 lb)
sauerkraut
⅛ l (4 fluid oz) sour
cream
1 tsp flour

Dice the pork into 1–2 oz pieces. Fry chopped onions and crushed garlic slightly brown, add paprika, meat and spices. Cover the meat with water, stew it app. 30 min. Add sauerkraut and cook until tender (app. 30 min.). Mix sour cream and flour, stir into the Goulash, allow to simmer for 5 min.

Serve with boiled potatoes, bread- or potato-dumplings.

Braised Mutton
Schöpsenbraten

1 kg (2 lb) mutton
(leg)
100 g (3½ oz) bacon
5 cloves of garlic
1 tsp salt
5 juniper berries
100 g (3½ oz) pot
herbs
(carrot, celeriac,
leek)
2 bay leafs
1 pinch rosemary
½ tsp thyme
5 pepper- and
5 pimento corns
1 Tbs vinegar

⅛ l (4 fluid oz) water
1 Tbs flour

Cut bacon in 1 cm thick and 3 cm long strips. Peel cloves of garlic. Cut holes in the meat and stuff them alternately with baconstrips and garlic cloves. Rub the meat with salt and crushed juniper berries. Heat the rest of chopped bacon in a saucepan, put in the meat. Fry over a good heat until it is brown all over. Fry chopped pot herbs in the same fat with the meat. Add spices and cover with water.
Braise uncovered in a hot oven app. 1 hour. Baste the meat frequently. Take the mutton out of the gravy, slice.
Mix water with flour, thicken the gravy ad sieve over the meat.

Serve with bread-dumplings and cabbage or salads.

Lamb with Lentils
Lammfleisch mit Linsen

800 g (1 ¾ lb) lamb
50 g (2 oz) cooking fat
100 g (3½) onions
1 clove garlic
1 tsp salt
1 pinch pepper
1 pinch rosemary
1 pinch thyme
⅛ l (4 fluid oz) white wine

Fry finely chopped onions and crushed garlic in fat until golden brown. Add diced meat. Fry. Stir in spices and wine and allow to stew in its own juice until it is almost done (¾ hours).

Cook soaked lentils with the spices.

Mix meat and lentils, cook until the meat is tender. Season and serve.

---

300 g (10 oz) lentils
1 bay leaf
1 pinch rosemary
½ tsp salt
1 Tbs vinegar

Roast Venison
Wildbraten

1 kg (2 lb) venison
(well hung)
(leg of stag or
roebuck)
100 g (3½ oz) bacon
½ tsp salt
10 juniper berries
½ tsp thyme

---

1 Tbs butter
50 g (2 oz) celeriac
50 g (2 oz) carrots
30 g (1 oz) turnips
50 g (2 oz) onions
2 cloves garlic
2 bay leafs
5 peppercorns
5 pimento corns
¼ l (8 fluid oz) red
wine
1 Tbs stewed
cranberries
60 g (2 oz) black
bread

Cut bacon in 1 cm thick and 4 cm long strips. Cut holes in the meat and stuff them with baconstrips. Rub the meat with salt, thyme and crushed juniper berries.

Heat butter and the remaining chopped bacon in a saucepan, fry the meat until it's brown all over. Fry finely chopped pot herbs, onions and garlic with the meat. Add wine, spices, cranberries, cubed bread. Roast in a hot oven app. 1½ hours. Baste the meat frequently. Add some water if necessary.

Cut the meat into slices and serve with the sieved sauce.

Red cabbage, bread- or potato-dumplings go well with it.

Paprika Chicken
Paprikahendl

1 chicken (app. 1,5 kg = 3 lb)
1 tsp salt
50 g (2 oz) butter
150 g (5 oz) onions
1 clove garlic
2 Tbs paprika
1 Tbs tomato-purée
¼ l (8 fluid oz) water or chicken stock

¼ l (8 fluid oz) sour cream
1 Tbs flour
½ tsp salt

Cut the chicken into pieces, salt and fry it all over in hot butter. Keep it warm. Fry finely chopped onions and crushed garlic in the same fat. Add paprika, tomato-purée, water or stock. Cook app. 5 min. Add the chicken pieces and simmer until tender (app. 30 min.).
Mix cream with flour, thicken the sauce, season and sieve over the served meat.

Side dishes: Nockerln or dumplings and green salad.

Minced Meat Balls
Faschierte Laibchen

500 g (1 lb) mince
(beef and pork
mixed)
50 g (2 oz) bacon
50 g (2 oz) onions
1 clove garlic
2 stale rolls
½ tsp marjoram
½ tsp basil
1 tsp salt
1 pinch nutmeg
1 tsp parsley
1 egg

----

fat for frying

Soak rolls in water, squeeze out and mash it. Fry chopped bacon, onions and crushed garlic until slightly brown. Mix in a bowl mince, rolls, egg and all the spices. Knead well until smooth. Shape balls (2 cm thick, diameter 7 cm). Fry slowly in hot fat until brown on both sides.

Serve with mashed potatoes, mixed salad or any vegetable.

Pilaf
Reisfleisch

*500 g (1 lb) veal or
lean pork
50 g (2 oz) lard
150 g (5 oz) onions
1 clove garlic
1 Tbs paprika
1 Tbs tomato-purée
1 tsp salt
½ l (1 pt) water
200 g (7 oz) rice*

grated cheese

Fry chopped onions and crushed
garlic in lard, add diced meat
and spices. Allow to stew in its
own juice app. 20 minutes. Remove 3 Tbs of juice. Add rice
and water and simmer for app.
20 min. Mix in the removed
juice, season and serve with
grated cheese and green salad.

Tyrolean Liver
Tiroler Leber

*500 g (1 lb) liver of
calf or pig
50 g (2 oz) bacon
40 g (1¾ oz) butter
40 g (1¾ oz) onions
1 Tbs flour
⅛ l (4 fluid oz) beef
stock
⅛ l (4 fluid oz) white
wine
1 pinch pepper
2 pinches marjoram
1 tsp salt*

Cut the liver in slices (1 cm
thick). Lard them with thin
strips of bacon. Fry finely chopped onions and liver slices in
butter. Sprinkle with flour, add
water, wine, spices (without
salt) and allow to simmer for 5
minutes. Salt and serve immediately.

Cooked potatoes or rice and lettuce go well with it.

Lights
Beuschel

1 kg (2 lb) calf's
lights
1½ l (3 pt) water
1 tsp salt
1 Tbs vinegar
100 g (3½ oz) pot
herbs
1 small onion
5 peppercorns
3 pimento corns
1 bay leaf
½ tsp thyme

---

60 g (2¼ oz) lard
60 g (2¼ oz) flour
1 tsp sugar
½ Tbs onions
1 tsp parsley
1 clove garlic
1 anchovy fillet
all finely chopped
½ l (1 pt) lights
stock

Cook lights slowly with coarse cut pot herbs and spices (app. 1½ hours). Preferably cook it a day before you wish to serve. Strain. Allow to get cold. Cut lights into thin strips (½ cm broad, app. 3–4 cm long). Remove all the gristle. Fry flour and sugar in lard brown, add chopped spices, fry for app. 2 min. Add lights stock, allow to cook for 10 min.

Mix in lights, season and simmer 10 min. Finally stir in sour cream.

1 tsp mustard
1 tsp lemon juice
½ tsp salt
½ tsp marjoram
⅛ l (4 fluid oz) sour
cream

It tastes best with bread-dumplings. In Tyrol they serve it also with Polenta.

Fried Brain Sandwiches
Hirnpofesen

250 g (9 oz) brain of
calf or pig

---

40 g (1¾ oz) butter
1 Tbs onions
1 tsp parsley
both finely chopped
2 eggs
1 tsp salt
2 pinches pepper

---

350 g (12 oz) stale
breakfast rolls

---

4 eggs
4 Tbs milk
½ tsp salt

---

fat for frying

Cut the rolls into 1 cm thick slices (app. 16 pieces). Wash the brain, cover with warm slightly sour (vinegar) water and allow to stand 10 min. Remove skin and veins and chop it up.
Fry onions and parsley for 2 minutes, add the brain, fry all together for app. 2 minutes. Whisk up eggs, add with spices to the brain, stir well until cooked. Spread the brain properly on half of breadslices, cover with the second half, press together.
Whisk up eggs, milk and salt, soak the sandwiches in it. Then fry in deep hot fat on both sides until golden brown.

Serve with spinach or salads. The fried sandwiches cut into 2 cm broad strips, can be also served with hot broth.

Burgenland Carp
Burgenländischer Karpfen

1 carp app. 1,2 kg
(2½ lb)
1 tsp salt
1 tsp paprika
50 g (2 oz) butter

---

150 g (5 oz) onions
1 clove garlic
2 Tbs paprika
⅛ l (4 fluid oz) white
wine
4 tomatoes
2 small slices
lemon rind
½ tsp salt

¼ l (8 fluid oz) sour
cream
1 Tbs flour

Scale, gut, wash the carp, cut into portions. Rub with salt and paprika, fry in hot butter. Keep it warm.
Fry chopped onions and crushed garlic in the frying fat. Add paprika, wine, peeled cubed tomatoes and spices. Allow to simmer ½ hour. Add mixed cream and flour, bring to boil, sieve it over the pieces of fish. Cook slowly app. 10 minutes.

Serve it with Nockerln or boiled potatoes and lettuce.

Trout with Herb Sauce
Forellen mit Kräutersoße

4 trout
1 lemon juice
1 tsp salt
3 Tbs flour
50 g (2 oz) butter

Sauce:
40 g (1¾ oz) butter
1 Tbs flour
¼ l (4 fluid oz)
beef stock
4 Tbs fresh,
chopped
herbs
(parsley, chervil,
sweet basil,
watercress)
⅛ l (4 fluid oz) sour
cream
1 egg yolk
½ tsp salt
1 pinch pepper

Scale, gut, wash the trout. Salt, sprinkle with lemon juice, dip in flour, fry in butter until brown. Keep it warm.

Sauce: Fry flour in butter until lightly brown, add stock, half the herbs and allow to cook for 10 minutes.

Mix egg yolk and cream, stir in the sauce, add herbs and spices. Reheat without boiling.

Serve this sauce with the trout with buttered potatoes and lettuce.

Other typical Austrian main courses

Stuffed Green Peppers
Gefüllte Paprika

8 green peppers
salted water

Stuffing:
400 g (14 oz) mince
(beef and pork
mixed)
1 Tbs lard
50 g (2 oz) onions
1 clove garlic
1 tsp parsley
1 tsp salt
½ tsp basil
½ tsp marjoram
2 pinches pepper
50 g (2 oz) cooked
rice
or 1 stale roll
1 egg

---

1 Tbs butter

---

tomato sauce (see
sauces)

Slice tops from peppers and re-move seeds. Pour boiling water over them, rinse with cold water. Scoop stuffing into the green peppers, replace the tops. Attach them with toothpicks. Place peppers upright in a but-tered saucepan. Pour tomato sauce over and cook until done (app. ½ hour).

Stuffing: Fry chopped onions and crushed garlic in lard. Mix mince, onions, chopped parsley, all spices, rice (or soaked, squee-zed roll) and egg.

Side dishes are: boiled or mashed potatoes.

Stuffed Savoy Cabbage
Gefüllter Kohl

1 Savoy cabbage,
medium
salted water

Stuffing:
400 g (14 oz) mince
(beef and pork mixed)
100 g (3½ oz) bacon
50 g (2 oz) onions
1 clove garlic
1 tsp parsley
½ tsp marjoram
½ tsp basil
1 pinch nutmeg
1 pinch pepper
1 tsp salt
1 stale roll
1 egg
cabbage heart

---

50 g (2 oz) bacon
¼ l (8 fluid oz)
beef stock

⅛ l (4 fluid oz)
sour cream
1 tsp flour
½ tsp salt
1 pinch pepper

Cook the cabbage head in salted water until half done. Allow to cool. Carefully loosen the leaves cut out the heart and chop it. Fill in the stuffing, spread also some stuffing between the leaves, tie with string.

Fry finely diced bacon in a tall saucepan, put in the cabbage head, add stock and braise until tender (app. 1 hour). Place cabbage onto a dish, keep warm. Mix cream and flour, thicken the sauce and pour it over the cabbage. Serve with boiled potatoes.

Stuffing: Mix in a bowl minced beef, finely shopped fried onions garlic and parsley, all the spices, the soaked squeezed out roll, egg and the chopped cabbage heart.

Baked Noodles with Ham
Gebackene Schinkenfleckerln

*200 g noodles
(squares)
salted water
1 Tbs oil*

---

*50 g (2 oz) butter
2 egg yolks
½ tsp salt
2 pinches pepper
and nutmeg
200 g (7 oz) cooked,
coarsly minced ham
4 Tbs sour cream
2 Tbs grated cheese
2 egg whites*

---

*fat and bread-
crumbs for the bak-
ing dish*

Cook the noodles in salted water
with oil, drain and set aside.
Beat butter and egg yolks until
fluffy. Stir in ham, spices, sour
cream, grated cheese and finally
fold in stiff whisked egg whites.
Grease an oven – proof dish,
sprinkle with breadcrumbs. Fill
in the noodle mixture and bake
in a moderate oven app. 40 min.
until golden brown.

Serve with salad.

Cabbage with Noodles (Squares)

Krautfleckerln

80 g (3 oz) lard
50 g (2 oz) onions
1 Tbs sugar
400 g (14 oz) cabb-age
1 Tbs vinegar
½ tsp caraway seeds
1 tsp salt
⅛ l (4 fluid oz) water

---

300 g (10 oz) noodles (squares)
salted water
1 Tbs oil

Fry finely chopped onions and sugar in lard until brown. Add thinly shredded white cabbage, spices, water and cook until done. Mix with the cooked, drained noodles.

Potato Goulash
Erdäpfelgulasch

1 kg (2 lb) potatoes
100 g (3 ½ oz) bacon
150 g (5 oz) onions
2 clove garlic
2 Tbs paprika
1 Tbs vinegar
1 tsp caraway-seeds
2 pinches marjoram
1 bay leaf
1 tsp salt
2 Tbs tomato-purée
app. ½ l (1 pt) water

Peel and cube raw potatoes (1 inch = 3 cm cubes). Fry finely chopped bacon, onions and crushed garlic until golden brown. Add paprika, vinegar, potatoes and spices and cover with water. Gently cook until the potatoes are done (app. 30 min.).
Finally thin slices of sausage can be added if desired.

Carinthian Cheese Dumplings
Kärntner Käsnudeln

*App. 16 medium
sized dumplings*

*Dough for
dumplings:
250 g (9 oz) flour
1 tsp salt
1 egg
6–8 Tbs milk or
water*

---

*Cheese-potato
filling:
500 g (1 lb)
potatoes
500 g (1 lb) chunky
cottage cheese or
curd
1 tsp salt*

Dough: Mix all ingredients in a bowl. Knead to a smooth elastic dough. Wrap in foil and allow to set for 2–3 hours. Roll out the dough on a floured board (2 mm thick). Place the filling balls on half of the dough, app. 4–5 cm (2 inch.) apart. Fold the other half of the dough over the filling. Press down dough very tightly on the balls. Cut out in semicircles. (Finally you can also squeeze the edges between thumb and forefinger in a special pattern ("krendln"). When all dumplings are worked out, drop them into boiling salt water and simmer for 10 min. (no longer!) Serve with melted butter.

Filling: Put the cottage cheese hours before preparing the dough in a sieve and let it drain, otherwise it will be too wet.

Cook potatoes, peel while hot and mash. Fry chopped leeks

50 g (2 oz) butter
50 g (2 oz) leeks
1 clove garlic
½ tsp mint
½ tsp chervil
½ tsp parsley
2 pinches marjoram

and crushed garlic for app. 5 min. in butter. Mix together hot potatoes, cottage cheese, leeks, chopped herbs and salt. Shape 16 balls.

Side dishes are: Green or cabbage salad.

Ritschert

Ritschert

250 g (9 oz) beans
250 g (9 oz) pearl
barley
1 small smoked
hand of pork
150 g (5 oz) celery
1 sage leaf
1 bay leaf
1 tsp allspice
salt

Soak beans and barley over-
night. Boil with meat and sea-
soning until almost done (app. 1
hour). Remove meat, bone and
cube it. Add meat, sliced celery
to the dish and stew until tender.

Vegetable Soufflé
Gemüseauflauf

500 g (1 lb) mixed vegetable in season salted water

---

1 Tbs butter
100 g (3½ oz) mushrooms

---

40 g (1¼ oz) butter
60 g (2 oz) flour
¼ l (8 fluid oz) milk
4 eggs
2 pinches nutmeg
1 tsp chopped parsley
2 Tbs grated cheese
100 g (3½ oz) chopped ham
½ tsp salt

---

butter and breadcrumbs for the baking dish

Wipe and dice vegetables, cook in little salted water until crunchy. Wipe and chop mushrooms, fry them in butter. Leave to cool.

Melt butter, add flour, cook for 2 minutes. Remove from heat, gradually stir in milk. Return to heat and stir until thickened. Allow to cool. Mix in egg yolks, cheese, ham, vegetable, mushrooms, spices and fold in stiff beaten egg whites.

Butter an oven-proof dish, sprinkle with breadcrumbs. Pour in the mixture, bake in a moderate oven app. 45 min. until golden brown.

Instead of fresh vegetables 350 g of frozen can be used.

Salads go well with it.

Cheese Spätzle
Käsespätzle

⅜ l (12 fluid oz)
water
1 tsp salt
1 spinch nutmeg
4 eggs
400 g (14 oz) flour

―――――――――

150 g (5 oz) grated
spicy cheese
1 pinch pepper
150 g (5 oz) onions
1 Tbs flour
2 pinches salt
fat for frying

―――――――――

30 g (1 oz) butter

Mix water, eggs, spices, fold in the flour. Immediately pass the dough through a coarse sieve into boiling salted water. Cook until the spätzle rise to the surface. Drain and rinse with warm water. Place in a large dish, alternating layers of spätzle with layers of cheese. Sprinkle the top with plenty of fried onion rings, pour on hot melted butter. For onion rings coat thin onion slices with salted flour and fry in hot fat.

Serve with salads.

Potato Doughnuts
Erdäpfelkrapfen

250 g (9 oz) cooked mashed potatoes
250 g (9 oz) flour
2 eggs
2 egg yolks
1 tsp salt
1 pinch nutmeg
50 g (2 oz) melted butter
30 g (1 oz) yeast
6 Tbs milk

Filling:
200 g (7 oz) minced ham
3 Tbs sour cream

---

fat for frying

Dissolve yeast in milk and mix into dough with the other ingredients. Roll it out on a floured board (½ cm thick). Cut into round shapes with a pastry cutter (diameter 2 inch.). Place a little heap of ham, mixed with sour cream on half the shapes. Use the other shapes to cover them. Press the edges together, cut out a second time. Fry the doughnuts in hot deep fat on both sides until golden brown.

Serve with salads or sauerkraut.

Cottage Cheese Dumplings
Topfenknödel

Method I:
250 g (9 oz) cottage
cheese or curd
2 eggs
2 stale rolls
100 g (3½ oz) semo-
lina
1 tsp salt

Method II.
The same ingre-
dients like above
and
100 g (3½ oz) bacon
1 Tbs chopped
chives
1 pinch nutmeg

Method I: Soak rolls in water, squeeze, pass through a sieve. Mix with other ingredients. Allow to rest 1–2 hours! Scoop out medium sized dumplings, drop in boiling salted water, simmer for 10 min.

Method II: Fry finely diced bacon and mix it with chives and nutmeg into the batter.

You may eat it with any vegetable, sauerkraut or salads. Prepared by method I you may roll them in breadcrumbs fried in butter. Then serve them with stewed fruit or damson jam.

Bread Dumplings
Semmelknödel

4 stale rolls
50 g (2 oz) fat
50 g (2 oz) onions
1 tsp parsley
1 tsp celery-leafs
4 Tbs flour
1 tsp salt
app. ¼ l (8 fluid oz)
milk
2 eggs

_____

salted water

Cut rolls into small cubes (1 cm). Fry chopped onions in fat until golden brown, add finely chopped parsley and celery leafs, fry for 1 min. Mix rolls, flour, onions, add milk, eggs, salt. Mix very well. Shape 8 dumplings, allow them to rest for ½ hour. Drop them into boiling salted water, simmer 10 min.

In different parts of Austria they mix into the dumpling-dough bacon, sausage, smoked meat or liver. Then these dumplings are called "Tyrolean Dumplings", "Liver Dumplings" ecc. Bread Dumplings are a main dish eaten with any vegetable or sauce. They also are eaten as side dish with meat or are served to beef broth.

Potato Dumplings
Erdäpfelknödel

750 g (1½ lb) pota-
toes
1 tsp salt
1 Tbs oil
150 g (5 oz) flour
50 g (2 oz) semolina
1 egg

salted water

Cook potatoes, peel and mash while hot. Sprinkle with salt and semolina, allow to cool. Lightly mix in flour, oil and egg. Knead together quickly. Shape 10 dumplings. Drop them in boiling salted water, simmer for 10 min.

They can be filled with cooked smoked ham, left-overs of meat, cracklings or fruit.
They can be eaten as a main course with any vegetable or sauce or as a side dish with meat.

Baked Bacon Dumplings
Gebackene Speckknödel

Potato dumplings dough:
Filling:
250 g (9 oz) bacon
1 Tbs chives
1 Tbs parsley
½ tsp paprika
2 pinches pepper and caraway-seeds

----

100 g (3½ oz) butter

¼ l (8 fluid oz) sour or fresh cream
1 egg

Ingredients and method see potato dumplings.
Filling: Dice bacon, mix with finely chopped chives, parsley and spices. Shape into little balls (diameter ¾ inch).
Form potato dumpling dough into a roll, cut to 12 pieces. Wrap in the filling balls. Dip each dumpling in melted butter. Place them side by side in a buttered pan an bake in a moderate oven golden brown (¾ hours). Mix egg and cream, pour over dumplings, allow to curdle (set).

Sauerkraut or warm Cabbage Salad go well with it.

Notices:

Snacks

Liptau Cheese
Liptauer Käse

250 g (9 oz) chunky cottage cheese or "Gervais" (originally Brimsen = smooth sheep cheese)
250 g (9 oz) butter
1 tsp paprika
½ tsp caraway-seeds
1 tsp chives
1 Tbs capers
1 anchovy fillet
1 tsp mustard

Chop caraway seeds, chives, capers and anchovy fillet very finely. Beat butter until fluffy, mix in cottage cheese and spices. Allow to stand 1 hour befor serving.

Meat Salad
Essigfleisch
1 portion

200 g (7 oz) cooked
cold beef
2 Tbs beef stock
2 Tbs vinegar
50 g (2 oz) onions
1 Tbs oil
1 pinch pepper
2 pinches salt

Cut the meat in thin slices, place them onto a plate. Mix stock and vinegar, pour over the meat. Allow to rest 1 hour.
Cut onions into thin rings and spread them over meat, add oil, pepper, salt.

In the same way you may prepare sausage or cold bread dumplings.

Mushrooms with Eggs
Schwammerln mit Ei

500 g (1 lb) wild
mushrooms (such
as chanterelles)
50 g (2 oz) butter
50 g (2 oz) onions
1 tsp parsley
1 tsp salt
2 pinches pepper

2 eggs

Wipe and wash mushrooms. Chop the large mushrooms coarsely, the small ones in half. Fry finely chopped onions in butter until golden brown, add chopped parsley, fry 1 minute. Stir in mushrooms, fry on a hot flame for app. 3 min. Season. Stir in beaten eggs, let them curdle. Sprinkle with chopped parsley and serve immediately.

Notices:

Side dishes —
Farinaceous —
Vegetables —
Salads — Sauces

Spätzle
Spätzle

300 g (10 ½ oz)
flour
1 tsp salt
1 egg
⅛ l (4 fluid oz) water

_____

salted water

_____

40 g (1¾ oz) butter

Mix flour, salt, water and egg until doughy. Immediately sieve the dough coarsely into boiling water. Cook 2 min., drain and rinse with cold water. Reheat in melted butter.

Nockerln
Nockerln

300 g (10½ oz) flour
1 tsp salt
50 g (2 oz) melted butter
2 eggs
⅛ l (4 fluid oz) milk

salted water

40 g (1¾ oz) butter

Mix all ingredients to a dough as for "Spätzle". Scoop out with a wet teaspoon into small, longish (app. 3 cm = 1 inch) dumplings (Nockerln), drop into boiling salted water, simmer for 3–4 min. Drain, rinse with cold water, reheat in melted butter.

Spätzle and Nockerln are popular side dishes with meat.

Fried Potatoes
Erdäpfelschmarrn

800 g (1¾ lb) pota-
toes
1 tsp salt
2 pinches caraway-
seeds
50 g (2 oz) fat
50 g (2 oz) onions

Cook floury potatoes, peel and slice them hot. Sprinkle with salt and crushed caraway-seeds. Fry chopped onions in fat until light brown, add potatoes and fry light brown. Turn often.

Riebel
Riebel

½ l (1 pt) milk
½ l (1 pt) water
1 tsp salt
170 g (6 oz)
semolina
170 g (6 oz) maize
meal

_____

50 g (2 oz) fat (lard)
30 g (1 oz) butter

Mix milk, water, salt, bring to boil. Trickle semolina mixed with maize meal into fluid. Allow to cook for 2 minutes and to become cold.

Heat fat in a pan, add the cooked mixture. Tear into small pieces with two forks. Fry it until golden yellow and crumbly. Finally add butter.

Riebel is very popular in Vorarlberg. They eat it for breakfast with milk or coffee. It is also a main dish served with stewed fruit or apple sauce.

Buckwheat Sterz
Heidensterz

400 g (14 oz) buck-
wheat flour
½ l (1 pt) water
1 tsp salt

---

50 g (2 oz) butter or
lard with cracklings

Stir the flour in a pan over a low heat until it is completly dry. Boil salted water, pour all the hot flour in the water, let it simmer for app. 10 min. Add hot fat and stir with a fork until the "Sterz" is crumbly.

Buckwheat Sterz is very popular in Carinthia and Styria. They eat it with milk or coffee for breakfast. It is also served with beef broth and mushroom soup.

Polenta
Polenta

1 l (2 pt) water
2 Tbs butter or lard
1 tsp salt
400 g (14 oz) maize
meal

Boil water with salt and fat. Trickle in maize meal, stirring all the time. Cook over a medium heat until the mixture loosens from the pan. Cook the Polenta covered in a medium oven (app. 30 min.).
Rinse a baking tin with cold water, press in Polenta, flip it out on a plate, cut in slices.

Mushroom Sauce
Schwammerlsoße

500 g (1 lb) mush-
rooms (any kind)
40 g (1½ oz) butter
50 g (2 oz) onions
1 clove garlic
½ tsp marjoram

⅛ l (4 fluid oz) sour
cream
1 Tbs flour
1 tsp parsley
1 tsp salt
1 pinch pepper

Wipe, wash and chop mush-
rooms. Fry finely chopped
onion, crushed garlic until light
brown, add mushrooms, marjoram, stew for 10 min.
Mix cream with flour, add to
mushrooms, cook for app. 2 minutes. Season with chopped
parsley, pepper and salt.

It tastes good with bread dumplings, fried potatoes or
buckwheat Sterz.

Cucumber Sauce
Gurkensoße

500 g (1 lb)
cucumber
40 g (1½ oz) butter
⅛ l (4 fluid oz) sour
cream
1 tsp flour
1 tsp salt
1 tsp dill

Slice or dice the peeled cucumber. Stew for app. 10 min. Mix cream with flour, add to cucumber, cook 2 minutes. Season with chopped dill and salt.

Serve with boiled beef and fried potatoes.

Dill Sauce
Dillsoße

40 g (1½ oz) butter
40 g (1½ oz) flour
⅜ l (12 fluid oz) beef
stock
10 Tbs dill
(2 bunches)
⅛ l (4 fluid oz) sour
cream
½ tsp salt

Fry flour in butter until golden brown, add stock, cook 15 min. Stir in finely chopped dill and sour cream, season. Reheat, but dont boil.

This is an excellent side dish with boiled beef and fried potatoes.

Tomato Sauce
Paradeissoße

750 g (1½ lb)
tomatoes
50 g (2 oz) onions
⅛ l (4 fluid oz) water
1 bay leaf

---

40 g (1½ oz) butter
1 Tbs sugar
40 g (1½ oz) flour
1 tsp salt

Cut tomatoes in small pieces, slice onions and cook with bay leaf in a little water until done (app. ½ hour). Sieve the mixture.

Fry flour and sugar with butter until golden brown, add tomato-purée salt and cook for 5 minutes.

Chive Sauce
Schnittlauchsoße

3 hard-boiled eggs
1 tsp mustard
½ tsp salt
2 pinches sugar
1 tsp lemon juice
⅛ l (4 fluid oz) oil

---

2 stale rolls
½ l (1 pt) vinegar
water
4 Tbs chives
4 Tbs sour cream

Remove the roll crusts. Soak the rolls in vinegar water, squeeze out and sieve. Sieve egg yolks, mix them with salt, sugar, mustard, lemon juice. Gradually stir in the oil. Mix in rolls, finely chopped chives, sour cream, sieved cooked egg whites.

Serve with boiled beef and fried potatoes.

Apple Horse-radish Sauce
Apfelkren

2 Tbs horse-radish
1 Tbs vinegar
1 pinch salt
1 tsp sugar
500 g (1 lb) apples

Peel and grate apples, mix with shredded horse-radish, season. Instead of raw apples, cooked sieved apples can be used.

Bread Horse-radish Sauce
Semmelkren

4 stale rolls
app. ⅜ l (12 fluid oz)
beef stock
½ tsp salt
2 pinches pepper
1 pinch nutmeg
4 Tbs horse-radish
1 Tbs vinegar
1 tsp butter or
1 Tbs fresh cream

Cut rolls into thin slices, pour hot beef stock over them. Allow to soak. Add shredded horse-radish, bring to boil. Remove from the heat, season, stir in butter or cream.

Horse-radish sauces are typical Austrian side dishes with boiled beef.

Viennese Beans
Fisolen auf Wiener Art

750 g (1½ lb)
French beans

---

40 g (1½ oz) butter
40 g (1½ oz) onions
1 clove garlic
40 g (1½ oz) flour
2 Tbs dill
1 tsp parsley
1 tsp salt
1 tsp vinegar
2 pinches pepper
⅛ l (4 fluid oz) sour
cream

Cut beans to pieces 1 inch = 3 cm long. Cover with water, cook until done. Fry finely chopped onions and crushed garlic for 2 min. in butter, add flour, fry until golden brown. Add to the beans, simmer for 10 min. Stir in finely chopped dill, parsley, sour cream and seasonings.

Savoy Cabbage
Kohlgemüse

500 g (1 lb) Savoy cabbage
200 g (7 oz) potatoes
1 tsp caraway seeds
2 clove garlic
1 cube beef stock

---

40 g (1½ oz) lard
40 g (1½ oz) flour
1 Tbs vinegar
½ tsp salt
2 pinches pepper

Cut cabbage into thin strips, peeled raw potatoes into cubes (1 inch = 3 cm). Add spices, cover with water and cook until done (app. 20 min.).
Fry flour in fat until brown, add to cabbage, simmer for 10 min. Season.

Good side dish with beef, pork and sausages.

Vegetable Marrow
Kürbisgemüse

600 g (21 oz)
vegetable marrow
1 tsp salt

---

40 g (1½ oz) lard
50 g (2 oz) onions
1 tsp paprika
1 Tbs tomato-purée
1 Tbs vinegar
1 tsp caraway-seeds

⅛ l (4 fluid oz) sour
cream
1 tsp flour

Peel the marrow, remove seeds, cut into long thin strips. Salt, allow to stand for ½ hour, then squeeze out.
Fry chopped onions in lard until lightly brown, add paprika, vinegar, marrow, tomato-purée, caraway-seeds. Stew for 20 min. Mix cream with flour, thicken the mixture.

Sauerkraut
Sauerkraut

500 g (18 oz)
sauerkraut
5 juniper berries
1 tsp caraway-seeds
1 apple

---

40 g (1½ oz) lard
40 g (1½ oz) onions
1 clove garlic
1 Tbs flour
salt as desired

Cook sauerkraut with the peeled quartered apple and spices in sufficient water to cover.
Fry finely chopped onions and crushed garlic for 2 min., add flour, fry until brown. Mix the roux with the sauerkraut, cook for 5 min., season.

Sauerkraut goes well with pork, sausages, dumplings and potatoes.

Cabbage with Tomatoes
Paradeiskraut

500 g (1 lb) white
cabbage
250 g (½ lb)
tomatoes

---

40 g (1½ oz) lard
40 g (1½ oz) onions
1 Tbs sugar
1 tsp salt
1 tsp paprika
½ tsp caraway-seeds

---

1 tsp flour
3 Tbs water

Shred cabbage, peel and quarter tomatoes.

Fry finely chopped onions and sugar until light brown. Add cabbage, spices and stew until tender. If necessary add a little water.

Mix flour and water, thicken the cabbage.

This is very good served with potato-dishes.

Stewed Red Cabbage
Gedünstetes Blaukraut

*600 g (21 oz) red
cabbage
2 Tbs vinegar*

---

*40 g (1½ oz) lard
40 g (1½ oz) onions
1 Tbs sugar
1 tsp salt
½ tsp caraway-seeds
4 cloves
1 apple
⅛ l (8 fluid oz) red
wine
ev. 10 chestnuts*

Shred the cabbage, mix immediately with vinegar so that the cabbage won't bleach.
Fry finely chopped onions and sugar until light brown. Add cabbage, spices, peeled sliced apple or chestnuts, wine and app. ⅛ l water. Stew until tender.

This is very good with venison, poultry, braised beef and dumplings.

Potato Salad
Erdäpfelsalat

750 g (1½ lb)
potatoes

⅛ l (4 fluid oz) beef
stock or water with
2 Tbs vinegar

---

50 g (2 oz) onions
4 Tbs vinegar
3 Tbs oil
1 tsp salt
2 pinches pepper

Boil potatoes, peel while hot, slice, moisten with beef stock or vinegar water. Add salt, pepper, vinegar, allow to cool. Mix in finely chopped onion and oil.

Finely chopped fresh herbs, mustard, sour cream or mayonnaise can also be mixed in.

Green (Lettuce) Salad
Grüner Salat

2 lettuce (app. 1 lb)

---

4 Tbs vinegar
1 tsp sugar
½ tsp salt
½ clove garlic
2 Tbs oil

Wipe, wash and divide lettuce. Mix vinegar with spices in a salad bowl, mix with salad. Now add oil.

This salad tastes good with chopped fresh herbs. In some parts of Austria they sprinkle the salad with hot, fried bacon bits.

Cucumber Salad
Gurkensalat

500 g (1 lb) cucumber
⅛ l (4 fluid oz) sour cream
2 Tbs vinegar
1 tsp salt
½ tsp caraway-seeds
½ clove garlic

Mix sour cream with spices in a bowl. Stir in peeled sliced cucumber. Serve immediately.
If required, the salad may be sprinkled with pepper, paprika or finely chopped dill or tarragon.

Beetroot Salad
Rohnensalat

500 g (1lb) beetroot

---

4 Tbs vinegar
4 Tbs water
½ tsp caraway-seeds
½ tsp anise
1 tsp salt
1 Tbs sugar

---

1 Tbs grated horse-radish
1 Tbs oil

Wash and cook beetroot (in pressure cooker 10–40 min., depending on the size). Put hot beetroot in cold water, skin, then slice.
Cook vinegar, water and spices for 2 min. strain hot liquid over beetroot. Allow to cool. Mix in horse-radish and oil.

Hot Cabbage Salad
Warmer Krautsalat

500 g (1 lb) white cabbage
½ l (1 pt) water
1 tsp caraway-seeds
1 tsp salt

---

100 g (3½ oz) bacon
salt and caraway-seeds as required
6 Tbs vinegar

Cook water with salt and caraway-seeds. Pour on shredded cabbage. Allow to stand for ½ hour, then strain.
Fry finely diced bacon until light brown, cook with vinegar and spices for 1 min. Pour over cabbage and mix well.

Traditionally served with roast pork, smoked meat or dumplings.

Hot Puddings and Sweets

Preparing Strudeldough
General instructions

Ingredients:
200 g (7 oz) flour
app. 8 Tbs warm water
½ tsp salt
½ tsp vinegar
1 Tbs oil

Method:
Mix all ingredients in a bowl, then knead on a board into a smooth, silky dough. Butter it, cover with a warm bowl and allow to sit for at least ½ hour. Spread a large soft cloth on a kitchen table, dust with flour and on it roll out the dough. Flour the hands. Work out the dough from the middle until it is paper thin. Cut off thick edges. Cover ¼ of the dough with filling, sprinkle the rest with melted butter. Fold over the edges. Roll the strudel up firmly (begin on the filled side). Roll it off the cloth on to a well greased baking tray. The join must be underneath. Brush the strudel with melted butter and bake in a medium oven ½–1 hour (this depends on the thickness). During baking brush now and again with melted butter.
Dust with sugar and serve either hot or cold.

Viennese Apple Strudel
Wiener Apfelstrudel

See general instructions for ingredients and method for dough.

Ingredients for filling:
50 g (2 oz) butter
100 g (3½ oz) breadcrumbs
1 kg (2 lb) apples
80 g (3 oz) sugar
1 tsp cinnamon
50 g (2 oz) raisins
50 g (2 oz) nuts
¼ l (8 fluid oz) sour cream

50 g (2 oz) melted butter

sugar

Method: Fry breadcrumbs in butter until light brown, allow them to cool. Peel and slice apples. Sprinkle ⅔ of the dough with breadcrumbs, place a thick layer of apples on it, sprinkle with sugar, cinnamon, raisins, chopped nuts. Spread sour cream on it. Brush the rest of the dough with melted butter. Roll up the strudel and bake in a moderate oven app. 45 min. Dust with sugar and serve either hot or cold.

Cottage Cheese Strudel
Topfenstrudel

See general instructions for ingredients and method for dough.

Ingredients for filling:

100 g (3½ oz) butter
100 g (3½ oz) sugar
3 egg yolks
500 g (1 lb) creamy cottage cheese or curd
1 tsp grated lemon rind
1 tsp vanilla sugar
2 tsp custard or maize flour
3 egg whites
1 pinch salt
50 g (2 oz) raisins

---

50 g (2 oz) melted butter

¼ l (8 fluid oz) milk

---

sugar

Method: Beat butter, sugar and egg yolks until fluffy. Add cottage cheese, spices, maize flour. Fold in stiff beaten egg whites. Proceed as for Cream Strudel. Serve with Vanilla Milk.

This strudel can also be baked on a baking tray like Apple Strudel. If done like Apple Strudel do not use milk.

Cream Strudel
Milchrahmstrudel

See general instructions for ingredients and method for dough.

Ingredients for filling:
4 stale rolls
¼ l (8 fluid oz) milk
100 g (3½ oz) butter
100 g (3½ oz) sugar
4 egg yolks
juice and rind of ½ lemon
1 tbs vanilla sugar
¼ l (8 fluid oz) sour cream
100 g creamy cottage cheese
4 egg whites
1 pinch salt
50 g (2 oz) raisins

¼ l (8 fluid oz) milk

---

50 g melted butter

---

sugar

Method: Remove the crust of the rolls. Soak rolls in milk, squeeze out and sieve. Beat butter, sugar, egg yolks and spices until fluffy. Add rolls, cream, cottage cheese and fold in stiff beaten egg whites.

Spread this mixture on ⅔ of the thin dough. Sprinkle with raisins, brush the rest of the dough with melted butter, roll up the strudel. Place it in a buttered oven-proof casserole dish and bake in a medium oven for app. 45 min. Half way through the baking time pour ¼ l boiling milk over the strudel and continue to bake.

Serve hot with Vanilla Milk.

Vanilla Milk
Vanillemilch

½ l (1 pt) milk
2 egg yolks
50 g (2 oz) sugar
1 Tbs vanilla sugar
1 tsp custard or
maize flour

Mix all ingredients together in a bowl. Whisk until creamy over a low heat without boiling.

These strudels are desserts, although they can be used as a main dish.

Fruit Dumplings
Obstknödel
Serve 4 as a main dish or 10 as a dessert.

Potato dough:
1 kg (2¼ lb) pota-
toes
1 tsp salt
250 g (8½ oz)
creamy cottage
cheese or curd
100 g (3½ oz) semo-
lina
150 g (5½ oz) flour
2 eggs
Filling:
1 kg (2¼ lb) fruits
eg. stoned apricot,
prunes, cherries,
bilberries
100 g (3½ oz) sugar
lumps

---

100 g (3½ oz) butter
100 g (3½ oz) bread
crumbs

---

sugar

Boil and peel potatoes while hot. Sieve and spread salt, curd and semolina on it. Allow to cool. Mix with flour and eggs. Knead together quickly. Form into a thick roll, cut into slices. Press out each slice. When stoned fruit used, then place a small lump of sugar. Wrap dough on it, shape dumplings, put into boiling salted water. Allow to simmer until the dumplings rise to the surface (app. 10 min.). Remove dumplings with a draining-spoon and roll in breadcrumbs fried in butter. Sprinkle with sugar and serve.

Rice Soufflé
Reisauflauf

½ l (1 pt) milk
¼ tsp salt
100 g (3½ oz) rice

50 g (2 oz) butter
50 g (2 oz) sugar
2 egg yolks
juice and grated
rind of ½ lemon
1 tsp vanilla sugar
50 g (2 oz) raisins
2 egg whites

butter and bread-
crumbs for the bak-
ing dish

Boil rice in salted milk, allow to cool. Cream butter, sugar and yolks. Mix in rice, spices and raisins. Fold in stiff beaten egg whites. Butter a baking dish, sprinkle with breadcrumbs. Add rice and bake in a medium oven for app. 45 min.
Another good method is to mix 250 g (8 ½ oz) cottage cheese or curd into the rice.
Serve hot with stewed fruit or raspberry juice.

Emperor's Omelette
Kaiserschmarrn

6 egg yolks
1 pinch salt
app. ¼ l (8 fluid oz)
milk or fresh cream
150 g (5 oz) flour
6 egg whites
50 g (2 oz) sugar

---

50 g (2 oz) butter
50 g (2 oz) raisins

---

sugar

Mix milk, salt, yolks and flour into a batter. Beat egg whites until stiff, beat in sugar spoon by spoon. Fold egg whites into batter.

Heat butter in a pan, pour in batter, sprinkle with raisins. Cover the pan with a lid and cook app. 3 min. over a medium flame until brown underneath. Turn the omelette and cook the second side until brown. Tear the omelette with two forks into little pieces.

Serve immediately dusted with sugar. Stewed fruit goes well with it.

102

Pancakes
Palatschinken
12 pieces

150 g (5 oz) flour
¼ l (8 fluid oz) milk
or ⅛ l (4 fluid oz)
cream and ⅛ l
(4 fluid oz) milk
2 eggs
2 egg yolks
¼ tsp salt
1 tsp sugar

fat for frying

jam for filling

sugar

Mix all ingredients into a thin batter.
Heat a little fat in a frying pan. Pour into the pan enough batter to cover the bottom thinly and evenly. Fry on both sides until golden brown. Grease the pan as before and continue until all the batter is used. Keep cooked pancakes warm. Spread each pancake with jam, roll it up and serve hot, dusted with sugar.

Salzburg Soufflé
Salzburger Nockerln
Serves 3

7 egg whites
1 pinch salt
2 Tbs fine granulated sugar
1 Tbs vanilla sugar
4 egg yolks
2 Tbs flour

_____

1 tsp butter
⅛ l (4 fluid oz) milk

_____

sugar

Beat egg whites with salt until stiff. Beat in sugar and vanilla. Carefully fold in yolks and flour. Heat butter in a shallow baking dish, add milk. Put in the mixture, shaped into 3 big dumplings. Bake in a medium oven app. 10 min. until golden brown. Dust with sugar and serve immediately.

Tipsy Lisl
Besoffene Lisl

4 egg whites
120 g (4½ oz) sugar
4 egg yolks
120 g (4½ oz)
breadcrumbs
1 Tbs flour
40 g (1½ oz) grated
hazelnuts
40 g (1½ oz) grated
cooking chocolate
½ tsp cinnamon
¼ tsp ground cloves
¼ tsp baking powder

---

butter and grated
hazelnuts for the
pudding bowl

¼ l (8 fluid oz)
mulled cider or wine

¼ l (8 fluid oz) fresh
cream

Beat egg whites until stiff. Beat in sugar spoon by spoon. Stir into egg yolks. Mix together all dry ingredients and fold them into the fluffy mixture.

Butter a bowl sprinkle with hazelnuts, fill with the mixture. Bake in a medium oven app. 45 min. Turn it on to a plate, pour over mulled cider or wine, allow to soak in.

Serve hot with whipped cream.

Mulled cider or wine: Heat the liquid with a small piece of cinnamon rind, lemon rind, some cloves and sugar es required. Dont boil!

This is a traditional dessert served at weddings in the countryside.

Coated Chocolate Pudding
Mohr im Hemd

100 g (3½ oz) butter
100 g (3½ oz) sugar
6 egg yolks
100 g (3½ oz)
grated cooking cho-
colate
100 g (3½ oz)
grated almonds
100 g (3½ oz) fine
breadcrumbs
6 egg whites

---

butter and sugar for
the pudding bowl

Chocolate sauce:
100 g (3½ oz)
cooking chocolate
100 g (3½ oz) sugar
³⁄₁₆ l (6 fluid oz)
water

¼ l (8 fluid oz) fresh
cream

Beat butter, half the amount of sugar and yolks until fluffy. Mix chocolate, almonds and bread-crumbs. Whisk egg whites until stiff, beat in the rest of sugar. Carefully fold into the mixture alternately the dry ingredients and beaten egg whites.

Butter a bowl, sprinkle with sugar, fill with the mixture. Steam the pudding 1 hour.

Turn on to a plate, coat with chocolate sauce, surround with whipped cream and serve hot.

Chocolate sauce: Bring diced chocolate, cold water and sugar to the boil. Stir well. Cook 5 min. pour hot over pudding.

Cold Desserts and Puddings
Pastries —
Cakes — Tarts

Carinthian Cake
Kärntner Reindling

Yeast dough:
500 g (1 lb) flour
10 g (⅓ oz) dried yeast or 30 g (1 oz) fresh yeast
80 g (3 oz) butter
¼ l (8 fluid oz) milk
1 egg
50 g (2 oz) sugar
1 tsp salt
½ tsb aniseeds

Filling:
50 g (2 oz) butter
100 g (3½ oz) sugar
2 Tbs cinnamon
100 g (3½ oz) raisins

---

50 g (2 oz) butter for baking tin

Yeast dough: Put the flour in a bowl. Mix in yeast (fresh yeast must be crumbled), sugar, salt, aniseeds. Melt butter, add milk, beat in the egg. (The liquid should be lukewarm.) Pour this mixture into the flour. Mix to a dough and beat hard for 10 min. Leave to rise in a warm place until double its original bulk. Place the dough on a floured board, knead well.

For this cake roll out the dough 1 cm (⅓ inch) thick. Brush with melted butter, sprinkle with sugar, cinnamon and raisins. Roll the dough up firmly. Place it in a well buttered round baking tin, rolled up like a snail's shell. Allow to stand in a warm place for app. ½ hour. Bake for 1 hour in a medium oven until golden brown. Allow to cool for 10 min. in the opened oven before turning out of tin.

In Carinthia Reindling will be eaten with coffee, or at Easter with cooked cold ham.

Fried Yeast Buns
Gebackene Mäuse

Yeast dough:
500 g (1 lb) flour
10 g (⅓ oz) dried
yeast
or 30 g (1 oz) fresh
yeast
50 g (2 oz) sugar
1 tsp salt
50 g (2 oz) butter
¼ l (8 fluid oz) milk
2 eggs
3 Tbs rum
100 g (3½ oz) rai-
sins

---

fat for deep frying

---

sugar

Mix all ingredients to a dough (see Carinthian Cake). Work raisins into the dough.
After rising scoop out little buns. Fry them floating in hot fat until golden brown all over. Allow to drain. Sugar and serve while warm.

Coffee, stewed fruit or raspberry juice go well with it.

Jam Buns
Buchteln

Yeast dough:
500 g (1 lb) flour
10 g (⅓ oz) dried
yeast
or 30 g (1 oz) fresh
yeast
60 g (2 oz) sugar
1 Tbs vanilla sugar
1 tsp grated lemon
rind
1 tsp salt
100 g (3½ oz) butter
1 Tbs rum
3 egg yolks
³⁄₁₆ l (6 fluid oz) milk

_____

250 g (8½ oz) jam

_____

100 g (3½ oz) butter

_____

sugar and 1 tsp
vanilla sugar

Prepare a yeast dough (see Carinthian Cake). After dough rises, knead it well on a floured board.

Roll it out in an oblong shape, 1 cm (⅓ inch) thick. Cut into squares (5 cm = 2 inch.). Place 1 teaspoon jam in the centre of each square. Wrap the dough round the jam. Dip each bun in melted butter and place close together on a well greased pan. Cover and put to rise until double the size. Brush with melted butter and bake in a medium oven until golden brown (app. 30–40 min.). Dust with sugar.

Serve with coffee or vanilla-milk (see Cream Strudel).

Marble Cake
Marmorkuchen

200 g (7 oz) butter
150 g (5 oz) sugar
1 Tbs rum
1 Tbs vanilla sugar
3 eggs
100 g (3½ oz) maize
or potato flour
250 g (8 ½ oz) flour
1 Tbs baking soda
⅛ l (4 fluid oz) milk
or sour cream
100 g (3½ oz)
cooking chocolate
or 3 Tbs cacoa
4 Tbs milk

---

fat and flour for the
mould

Beat butter, sugar, eggs and spices until fluffy. Mix in flour, baking soda and milk. Put half of this mixture in another bowl. If chocolate is used, melt it in hot milk, if cocoa, mix with lukewarm milk. Mix into half of the mixture. Grease and flour a baking tin. Fill in alternately dark and yellow dough. Bake in a medium oven app. 1 hour. Allow to cool before turning out of the mould. Dust with sugar.

Emperor's Guglhupf
Kaiserguglhupf

140 g (5 oz) butter
140 g (5 oz) sugar
4 egg yolks
8 Tbs lukewarm milk
1 Tbs vanilla sugar
1 tsp grated lemon rind
1 Tbs rum
280 g (10 oz) flour
1 tsp baking soda
50 g (2 oz) raisins
4 egg whites

---

butter and flour for the mould

Beat butter, sugar, egg yolks and spices until fluffy. Stir in milk, flour mixed with baking soda and raisins little by little. Carefully fold in stiff beaten egg whites. Place the mixture in a buttered, floured mould (there is a special shape, but any ring mould will do). Bake in a medium oven app. 45 min. until golden brown. Allow to cool before turning out. Dust with sugar.

Brown Cherry Cake
Brauner Kirschkuchen

200 g (7 oz) butter
150 g (5 oz) sugar
4 egg yolks
1 Tbs rum
1 Tbs vanilla sugar
1 Tbs sour cream
200 g (7 oz) flour
150 g (5 oz) grated almonds
150 g (5 oz) grated cooking chocolate
4 egg whites
1 pinch salt
50 g (2 oz) sugar

---

1 kg (2 lb) cherries

---

fat and flour for baking tray

---

sugar

Beat butter, sugar, egg yolks, spices and sour cream until fluffy. Mix flour with almonds and chocolate. Whisk egg whites with salt until stiff. Beat in sugar little by little. Fold flour and beaten egg whites alternately into butter mixture.
Remove stems from cherries, wash and dry them, roll in flour. Grease and flour a baking tray. Spread cake mixture 1 cm (½ inch) high on the tray, sprinkle with cherries and bake in a hot oven app. ½ hour. Allow to cool, dust with sugar.

Walnut Roll
Nußrolle

4 egg yolks
100 g (3 ½ oz) sugar
120 g grated nuts
1 Tbs flour
4 egg whites
1 pinch salt
2 Tbs sugar

Filling:
¼ l (8 fluid oz) fresh cream
1 tsp vanilla sugar

---

grease-proof paper

Beat yolks and sugar until fluffy. Mix flour and nuts. Whisk egg whites with salt until stiff, beat in sugar. Fold nuts and beaten egg whites alternately into mixture.

Line the baking tray with grease-proof paper. Spread the mixture on it (1 cm = ½ inch high). Bake in a hot oven app. 15 min. Roll it up with the paper, allow to cool. Remove the paper. Spread the filling on the cake, roll up again, dust with sugar.

Filling: Whip the cream until stiff. Stir in vanilla sugar.

Chocolate Roll
Schokoladerolle

6 egg yolks
80 g (3 oz) sugar
50 g (2 oz) grated
almonds
120 g (4 oz) melted
chocolate
6 egg whites
1 pinch salt
1 Tbs sugar

Filling:
100 g (3½ oz) red
current jam
¼ l (8 fluid oz) fresh
cream
1 tsp vanilla sugar

---

grease-proof paper

Melt the chocolate first. Beat yolks and sugar until fluffy. Mix in chocolate. Whisk egg whites with salt until stiff, beat in sugar. Fold almonds and beaten egg whites alternately into mixture.

Line the baking tray with grease-proof paper. Spread the mixture on it (1 cm = ½ inch high). Bake in a hot oven app. 15 min. (preheat the oven) Roll it up with the paper, allow to cool. Remove the paper. First Spread the jam, then the whipped, sugared cream on the cake, roll up again, dust with sugar.

Linz Tart
Linzer Torte

200 g (7 oz) flour
120 g (4 oz) butter
120 g (4 oz) grated nuts
100 g (3½ oz) sugar
1 tsp cinnamon
2 pinches ground cloves
½ tsp grated lemon rind
1 Tbs lemon juice
1–2 Tbs fresh cream
1 egg
1 egg yolk

---

1 egg white to brush
1 Tbs almond flakes

---

250 g (8½ oz) red current jam

Spread flour on a board, cut the butter in it, rub with the fingers until the mixture looks like fine breadcrumbs. Mix in all dry ingredients and knead with eggs, cream and lemon juice quickly to a dough.

Fill the cake-mould with ¾ of the dough, spread on the jam. Shape fingerthick rolls out of the rest of the dough. Arrange them in a lattice over the mixture in the mould. Brush the lattice with egg white, sprinkle with almond flakes. Bake the tart in a medium oven app. 50 min.

Do not cut until the next day.

Walnut Tart
Nußtorte

7 egg yolks
100 g (3½ oz) sugar
160 g (5⅔ oz)
grated walnuts
1 Tbs flour
7 egg whites
1 pinch salt
60 g (2 oz) sugar

---

4 Tbs rum

---

100 g (3½ oz) red
current jam
½ l (1 pt) fresh
cream

---

walnut kernels to
decorate

Beat yolks and sugar until fluffy. Mix nuts and flour. Whisk egg whites with salt until stiff. Beat in sugar spoon by spoon. Fold nuts and beaten egg whites alternately into yolk mixture.

Grease and flour a cake mould (Ø 18 cm). Fill in the mixture and bake in a medium oven app. 1 hour (preheat the oven). Allow to cool.

Cut off the top of the tart (one finger thick), place to one side. Hollow out the remainder of the tart. Take hollowed out portion and crumble it. Mix the crumbs with rum and half of the whipped cream. Re-stuff this mixture into the hollowed out tart and cover again with the top, previously removed.

Spread the tart thinly with jam, then coat with whipped cream. Decorate with walnut kernels and whipped cream.

Sacher Tart
Sachertorte

140 g (5 oz) butter
120 g (4 oz) sugar
180 g (6 oz) melted
cooking chocolate
8 egg yolks
140 g (5 oz) flour
8 egg whites
40 g (1½ oz) sugar

---

100 g (3½ oz)
apricot jam

---

chocolate icing:
200 g (7 oz) sugar
⅛ l (4 fluid oz) water
150 g (5 oz) cook-
ing chocolate
1 tsp butter

Beat butter and sugar until fluffy. Stir in chocolate. Beat in egg yolks little by little. Whisk egg whites until very stiff. Beat in sugar spoon by spoon. Fold flour and egg whites alternately into butter mixture.

Grease and flour a cake mould. Fill in the mixture and bake slowly for 1½ hours (150° C = 238° F). Turn out on to a cake rack and allow to cool. Glaze the top of the tart with hot jam and cover with chocolate icing.

Chocolate icing: Melt chocolate with butter in a double boiler. Cook sugar and water for 10 min. Stir chocolate and butter until smooth. Stir hot sugar water spoon by spoon into chocolate until completely blended. Spread immediately over the tart.

Sacher Tart is eaten with whipped cream.

Cottage Cheese Tart
Topfentorte

Sponge cake:
3 eggs
90 g (3 oz) sugar
½ tsp grated lemon rind
90 g (3 oz) flour
1 pinch baking soda
1 Tbs melted butter

Cream:
500 g (1 lb) creamy cottage cheese or curd
2 lemon juice
1 tsp grated lemon rind
100 g (3½ oz) sugar
1 Tbs vanilla sugar
3 tsp powered gelatine
6 Tbs water
¼ l (8 fluid oz) fresh cream

Sponge cake: Beat eggs and sugar in a bowl, standing in hot water. Beat until the mixture is thick and light. Fold in flour, mixed with baking soda, then fold in carefully melted butter. Grease and flour a baking mould. Fill in the mixture and bake in a medium oven app. 20 min. Allow to cool in the mould. Spread with cream and leave to set in the refrigerator.

Cream: Dissolve gelatine in hot water. Mix cottage cheese, sugar and lemon, stir in liquid gelatine. Fold in whipped cream.

Cottage Cheese Tartlets
Topfentascherln

150 g (5 oz) butter
150 g (5 oz) flour
150 g (5 oz) low fat
cottage cheese or
curd
2 pinches salt

100 g (3½ oz)
apricot jam

1 egg white for
coating

Spread flour on a board, cut the butter in it. Rub with the fingers until the mixture looks like fine breadcrumbs. Mix in sieved cottage cheese and salt. Knead quickly to a dough.

Allow to set for 1 hour in the refrigerator. Roll out the dough 2 mm thick, cut into squares (8 cm, 2½ inch). Place 1 teaspoon jam in the centre of each square, brush edges with egg white. Fold into poach shaped tartlets, brush with egg whites. Place on a baking tray, bake in a hot oven until golden brown (Preheat the oven). Dust with sugar and serve lukewarm.

The tartlets can also be filled with cooked, chopped ham.

Vanilla Crescent
Vanillekipferln

200 g (7 oz) butter
250 g (8½ oz) flour
100 g (3½ oz) pee-
led, grated almonds
1 Tbs vanilla sugar
50 g (2 oz) sugar
1 egg yolk

---

100 g (3½ oz) sugar
1 Tbs vanilla sugar
to roll in

Spread flour on a board, cut butter in it, rub with the fingers until the mixture looks like fine breadcrumbs. Mix in all dry ingredients and knead with the yolk quickly to a dough. Allow to set for ½ hour in the refrigerator. Shape rolls, cut off small pieces. Shape them into crescents. Place on a baking tray and bake in a medium oven until light brown. Roll in sugar, mixed with vanilla sugar.

Ischl Cakes
Ischler Törtchen

250 g (8½ oz) butter
250 g (8½ oz) flour
120 g (4 oz) peeled
grated almonds
120 g (4 oz) sugar
1 pinch cinnamon
1 Tbs lemon juice

Filling:
200 g (7 oz) apricot
or red current jam

---

sugar

Spread flour on a board, cut butter in it, rub with the fingers until the mixture looks like fine breadcrumbs. Mix in all dry ingredients and knead with lemon juice quickly to a dough. Allow to set for ½ hour in the refrigerator.

Roll out the dough 2 mm thick. Cut out circles with a pastry cutter (⌀ 5 cm, 2 inch). Cut 3 small holes in each second circle. Bake in a medium oven until lightly brown. Allow to cool. Dust perforated circles with sugar. Spread jam on plain circles, and place perforated circles on top.

Gingerbread
Lebkuchen

100 g (3½ oz) honey
4 eggs
400 g (14 oz) sugar
1 Tbs cinnamon
½ tsp ground ginger
½ tsp ground cloves
½ tsp ground pimento
1 pinch ground nutmeg
1 tsp grated lemon rind
1 lemon juice
50 g (2 oz) grated almonds
600 g (21 oz) rye flour
1½ tsp bicarbonate of soda

---

1 egg for coating

---

almond flakes to decorate or sugar icing.

---

baking wax

Mix eggs, honey, sugar and spices, stir in flour mixed with bicarbonate of soda and grated almonds. Knead to a dough quickly. Roll out the dough (6 mm = ¼ inch thick). Cut out different shapes with pastry cutters. Brush gingerbread with egg. If desired decorate with almond flakes. Place on a waxed baking tray and bake in a hot oven until medium brown.

If desired coat with sugar icing. Sugar icing: Mix 300 g (10½ oz) sugar with ½ egg white and app. 4 Tbs boiling water. Stir until it becomes a thick white icing.

Snowballs
Schneenockerln
Serves 4

4 egg whites
150 g (5½ oz) sugar

¾ l (1½ pt) milk
1 Tbs vanilla sugar

Vanilla sauce:
½ l (1 pt) milk
1 Tbs custard or
maize flour
100 g (3½ oz) sugar
1 Tbs vanilla sugar

---

2 egg yolks
4 Tbs fresh cream

⅛ l (4 fluid oz) whipped fresh cream

Whisk egg whites until stiff. Beat in sugar spoon by spoon. The mixture must be very stiff. Bring milk and vanilla sugar to the boil. Scoop large spoonfuls out of the egg whites (8 pieces) and drop into the milk. Let the "Nockerln" simmer on each side for 2 min. Remove and allow to drain. Place on a dish, cover with vanilla sauce and decorate with whipped cream.

Vanilla sauce: Strain the remains of the milk in which the "Nockerln" were cooked. Bring ½ l (1 pt) milk with sugar and vanilla to a boil. Stir in dissolved custard, cook for 2 min.
Stir yolks and cream until blended. Whisk this mixture into vanilla milk. Allow to cool.

Contents

Other typical Austrian main courses

Snacks

Side dishes – Farinaceous – Vegetables Salads – Sauces

Hot Puddings and Sweets

Cold Desserts and Puddings Pastries Cakes – Tarts